GET STUFF DONE

A Guide to Managing Your Time and Being Productive

Terri Dougherty

© 2024 ReferencePoint Press, Inc.
Printed in the United States

For more information, contact:
ReferencePoint Press, Inc.
PO Box 27779
San Diego, CA 92198
www.ReferencePointPress.com

ALL RIGHTS RESERVED.
No part of this work covered by the copyright hereon may be reproduced or used in any form or by any means—graphic, electronic, or mechanical, including photocopying, recording, taping, web distribution, or information storage retrieval systems—without the written permission of the publisher.

LIBRARY OF CONGRESS CATALOGING-IN-PUBLICATION DATA

Names: Dougherty, Terri, author.
Title: Get stuff done : a guide to managing your time and being productive
 / Terri Dougherty.
Description: San Diego, CA : ReferencePoint Press, Inc., [2024] | Includes
 bibliographical references and index.
Identifiers: LCCN 2023019003 (print) | LCCN 2023019004 (ebook) | ISBN
 9781678206048 (library binding) | ISBN 9781678206055 (ebook)
Subjects: LCSH: Time management--Juvenile literature.
Classification: LCC BF637.T5 D68 2024 (print) | LCC BF637.T5 (ebook) |
 DDC 155.4/19--dc23/eng/20230501
LC record available at https://lccn.loc.gov/2023019003
LC ebook record available at https://lccn.loc.gov/2023019004

CONTENTS

Introduction   **4**
Managing It All

Chapter One   **7**
Why Is It Tough to Get Stuff Done?

Chapter Two   **17**
Taking Control

Chapter Three   **25**
Do It Today

Chapter Four   **34**
Dealing with Distraction

Chapter Five   **44**
Overcoming Procrastination

Source Notes   53
For Further Research   56
Index   59
Picture Credits   63
About the Author   64

INTRODUCTION

Managing It All

Emerson is a typical teen with a packed schedule. After the sixteen-year-old gets home from school, she does her homework, feeds the family's cats, makes some dinner, and heads to a two-hour swim team practice. It's a tight schedule, but sticking to a routine helps Emerson make sure everything gets done. "Before I go to swim practice, I have to eat dinner and make sure I finish any homework because I get home kind of late,"[1] she says.

There is no shortage of obligations, pressures, and chaos coming at teens. Homework, sports, after-school clubs, youth groups, chores, a part-time job, family, and friends are all vying for a teen's time. Teens need to make sure they get to places on time, have all their assignments turned in, and spend time with the people who play important roles in their lives. They need to take control of the mayhem and make sense of what's coming at them. To get stuff done, they need to manage their time. There are tips, tricks, and skills that can help, but teens also need to be aware of the disruptions and procrastination traps that can steal their time and productivity.

The Social Media Allure

Today's teens are dealing with distractions that previous generations didn't have to worry about. Smartphones offer the opportunity to be constantly connected to the latest news, trends, and gossip, and they can be incredibly addicting. It's easy to become trained to associate a phone notification with the positive feeling that comes with seeing a post that's new, exciting, and interesting.

Once a teen picks up a smartphone, it's tough to put it down. Social media scrolling and text messages can be a constant source of distraction, offering an easily accessible and enjoyable alternative to any task. A 2021 survey published in *Education Sciences* found that 67 percent of teens believe that smartphones are hurting their ability to concentrate.

As more distractions have crept into our lives, our attention span has dwindled. Gloria Mark, a professor at the University of California, studies how technology affects workers and found that people now spend much less time working on a single task. In 2004, her researchers timed people with stopwatches to see how long they spent doing one thing, such as working on a Word document, before switching to something else, such as checking their email. They found that workers spent about two and a half minutes working on a task before switching. They studied workers again in 2012 and used computerized methods to find out how long people worked on one task. This time, they found that they spent about seventy-five seconds. The study was conducted again in 2020 and found that workers spent about

> "Our attention spans while on our computers and smartphones have become short—crazily short."[2]
>
> —Gloria Mark, a professor at the University of California

There is no shortage of obligations, pressures, and chaos coming at teens. Homework, sports, after-school clubs, youth groups, chores, a part-time job, family, and friends are all vying for a teen's time.

forty-seven seconds doing one thing before switching to another task. "Our attention spans while on our computers and smartphones have become short—crazily short,"[2] Mark explains.

Constantly switching from task to task is common but not good, Mark says. Being interrupted causes stress to increase and makes work take more energy. In addition, switching between tasks makes people more prone to errors and ends up making work take longer. "There's something called a switch cost," she explains. "So every time you switch your attention, you have to reorient to that new activity, that new thing you're paying attention to, and it takes a little bit of time."[3]

Overcoming Impulses

Digital distractions such as phone notifications make it extremely difficult to focus and concentrate when studying for an exam, writing a report, or reading a book. They are especially compelling because of the way our brains are wired. Teens are primed to react to things that grab their attention and are intrigued by something new. Teens also have biology working against them; the part of the brain that controls impulses is still developing. That makes it tougher to avoid picking up a smartphone when you should be studying.

In addition, we tend to think things will take us less time than they actually will. It might seem like a reading assignment should only take half an hour, so you spend a few hours playing video games before starting. When you finally get around to reading the assignment, you find that you've barely managed to finish half of the assignment in the amount of time you thought it would take to finish it. Your optimistic time estimate could end up costing you some sleep—or cause you to leave your homework unfinished.

Although time management may not come naturally, time management skills can be learned. Strategies can help you stop procrastinating and wasting time. By making the best use of your time, you can become more productive and have more time to do things you enjoy.

CHAPTER ONE

Why Is It Tough to Get Stuff Done?

Seventeen-year-old Autumn is a senior in high school. She manages a busy schedule that includes tennis, an after-school board game club, and a part-time job at a local horse farm. She also attends to her schoolwork and household chores. She learned the hard way that to get it all done, she had to learn to manage her time. "A couple of years ago I had some big projects due, and I waited until the last minute," she recalls. "I had to cram it all into one night."[4]

The stress that comes when rushing to finish a project at the last minute is probably familiar to you. At one point or another, virtually everyone feels like there is just too much to do and too little time to do it. Deadlines for homework can sneak up on you, assignments can pile up, and a college or scholarship application that isn't due for months can easily be put off until the last minute. There's a lot going on, and it's tough to figure out how to juggle school, homework activities, and other responsibilities and still have time to just relax.

Brain Battle: Impulsive Pleasure Versus Long-Term Gain

The challenge of getting stuff done is rooted in human biology. Time management problems don't start with a mountain of homework or a packed schedule, but with the brain. The part of the

> "A couple of years ago I had some big projects due, and I waited until the last minute. I had to cram it all into one night."[4]
>
> —High school senior Autumn

brain that craves immediate rewards is often at war with the part that is looking out for our long-term good.

The limbic system is the emotional and impulsive part of our brain that entices us to do what feels good in the moment. It loves immediate sensations and lives for the now. The brain's prefrontal cortex is more patient. It is where thoughtful decisions and plans are made and the importance of future goals is understood. It's the part of the brain that focuses on the abstract and the big picture.

Although all people have similar brain structure, these parts of the brain develop at different rates. The limbic system develops more quickly, whereas the prefrontal cortex takes much longer. In teens, the prefrontal cortex is still growing, and it doesn't finish developing until they're in their twenties. Because of this, the teen brain can find it difficult to prioritize working on something with a distant deadline over something that provides immediate pleasure. The stress and anxiety that come with working on something at the last minute is remote, but the gratification of having fun with your friends is here right now.

The Impact of Sleep

Sleep, or the lack of it, can also play a role in the impulsivity of the brain. When the brain's prefrontal cortex is tired, it's more difficult to resist the temptation of an immediate reward. Just as your muscles get tired when you repeatedly lift weights, the prefrontal cortex gets tired of saying no. When it's well rested, it has the strength to help you understand the consequences of an impulsive choice, like picking up your phone rather than doing homework, and make better long-term decisions.

It's not easy for teens to get enough sleep, however. The American Academy of Sleep Medicine recommends teens get eight to ten hours of sleep each night, but only about a third of teens get this amount. One reason it's tough for teens to get enough sleep is that their natural sleep/wake schedule doesn't match their school schedule. During the teen years, the body's sleep drive builds more slowly, and teens don't start to feel tired until late in the evening. In addition, in teens, the hormone melatonin isn't produced until late at night. This is the hormone that helps promote sleep. "Teens have the unique challenge of a biological shift in their circadian clock, causing them to struggle to fall asleep before 11 p.m.," explains Dr. Caroline Okorie, a sleep specialist. "Many teens will stay up late but still have to wake up early the next morning for school."[5]

Electronic devices also play a role in teen sleep deprivation. After doing four or five hours of homework at night, many teens turn to their phones as a way to wind down. "It's nice to stay up and talk to your friends or watch a funny YouTube video," one teen comments. "There are plenty of online distractions."[6] Electronic devices can be detrimental for sleep, however, as they stimulate

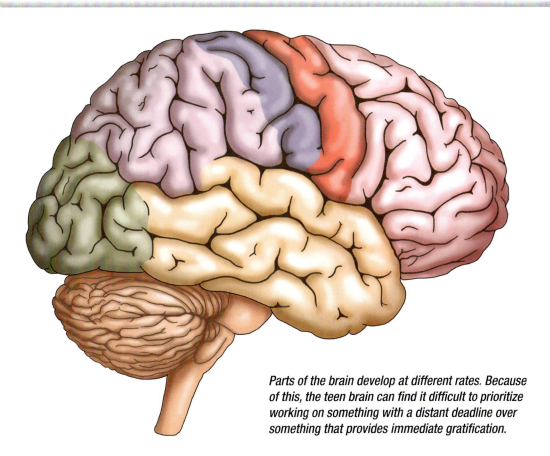

Parts of the brain develop at different rates. Because of this, the teen brain can find it difficult to prioritize working on something with a distant deadline over something that provides immediate gratification.

the body to stay awake. The light from a screen can cause problems with the production of melatonin, and notifications, texts, and calls can disrupt sleep.

This affects your productivity. A lack of sleep affects your ability to pay attention, makes you irritable, and more likely to be anxious and depressed. Getting enough rest, on the other hand, helps memory and your ability to analyze information. In addition, it helps you think more creatively.

Sweet Dreams

The Sleep Foundation recommends putting away electronic devices for at least half an hour before bed and silencing them so you don't check them during the night. If it's tempting to pick up your phone when it's next to your bed, you could put the phone in another room at night and use an alarm clock rather than your phone's alarm to wake you up.

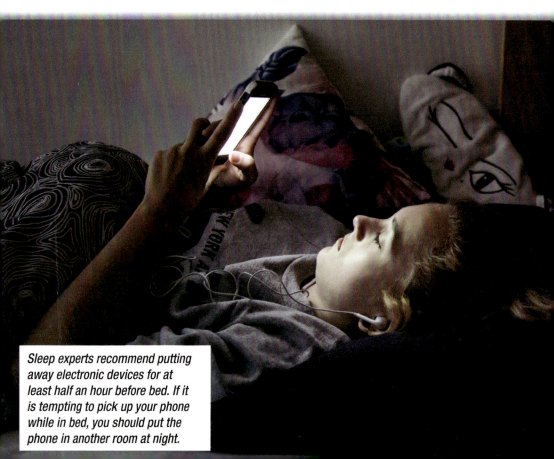

Sleep experts recommend putting away electronic devices for at least half an hour before bed. If it is tempting to pick up your phone while in bed, you should put the phone in another room at night.

Letting Go

Sometimes there are simply too many things vying for your time. When that happens, you need to make a thoughtful, yet tough, decision.

Autumn, a high school senior, faced a tough choice when she couldn't make time for tennis, a part-time job at a horse farm, and a youth group. "I used to be very involved in church youth group, but between work, school, and tennis in the fall I didn't have time to be part of the youth group, so I took a step back and sacrificed that for some of the other things," she explains. "It is really hard, but I weigh the positives and negatives of each."

When making her choice, she reasoned that the horse farm was understaffed, whereas the youth group had more people who were willing to volunteer. In addition, after the fall tennis season ended, she could return to the youth group.

Autumn, interview with the author, March 5, 2023.

In addition, to sleep well, avoid caffeine in the afternoon and evening and follow a relaxing nighttime routine. You can wind down with a few stretches or relaxing music. Simple things, like putting on your pajamas and brushing your teeth, can signal your body that it's time to rest. In addition, try to go to bed and get up at roughly the same time each day, and keep your bedroom cool, dark, and quiet.

For optimal rest, budget at least eight hours of sleep into your daily schedule. Emerson has dinner and does homework before swim team practice, which lasts from 6:30 to 8:30 p.m. "When I get home, I take a shower and go right to bed,"[7] she says. This way, she can get a decent night of sleep and make it to school by the 8 a.m. start time.

Eating Right

Your diet also affects your ability to be engaged with your work, get organized, and concentrate on what you need to do. Food is fuel, and when you're not giving your body the right fuel, it's tough to have the energy to do your best work. A study published in the *British Journal of Health Psychology* looked at how eating fruit, vegetables, sweets, and chips impacted the well-being, curiosity, and creativity of young adults. It found that on days when young adults ate more fruits and vegetables, they reported being happier, more curious, and more creative.

It often takes conscious effort to make healthier food choices. A hectic schedule can make it difficult to make healthy eating a priority, and the stress of looming deadlines can impact the foods that appeal to you. When you're under stress, your body releases hormones that make you crave foods that are high in fat and sugar. However, these foods can wreak havoc with your blood sugar levels and impact your energy level and mood. When blood sugar levels get too high, a foggy brain may make it difficult to focus. When they fall, you can feel crabby.

In general, it's best to choose foods with more nutrients and fiber and fewer fats and sugars. When you're ready for a snack, reach for apples, bananas, avocado slices, nuts, or whole grain toast with peanut butter rather than candy bars, sugary cereals, or granola bars. Healthier foods will help you feel full longer and will support a healthier weight and overall better health.

In addition, avoid the temptation to consistently use caffeine and energy drinks to carry you through your homework sessions. The blogger Kamogelo notes on the *Voices of Youth* blog that she had prioritized productivity at the expense of her health. "I was addicted to energy drinks and coffee because I was depriving myself of sleep so I could do more with schoolwork," she says. "I was constantly tired, constantly sick and I could feel my body becoming weaker." She would get only three hours of sleep each night, she said. "I would find myself constantly exhausted because I felt as though I wasn't doing enough and had to work more."[8]

Once Kamogelo allowed herself to rest, stopped drinking energy drinks, and took care of her health, she found that she did better academically. "That was the term I did the best academically and that's because I took care of myself and my health above all else,"[9] she asserts.

Don't Let Perfectionism Hold You Back

If you're a perfectionist, you might find it tough to begin a project. When faced with a challenge, you might be worried that you won't excel, and the end result won't meet your own high standards. You might also worry that your work will be criticized. "That fear of failing, that fear of it not being good enough or not pleasing others can be enough to put you off ever even starting it," comments psychology professor Fuschia Sirois of Durham University.

To get started, set a reasonable goal. Break the project into manageable pieces, and take things one step at a time. Concentrate on each step rather than worrying about making the end product perfect. Congratulate yourself for reaching each milestone, and give yourself permission to make mistakes. If you need help along the way, don't be shy about asking for it. "Write down what you need support with right now, and next to that write at least one person who can help you with that task," suggests Briana Mary Ann Hollis, a life coach and higher education professional. "This will show you that you don't have to do everything by yourself."

Quoted in Kim Mills, "Why We Procrastinate and What to Do About It, with Fuschia Sirois, PhD," *Speaking of Psychology* (podcast), Episode 210, American Psychological Association, October 2022. www.apa.org.

Quoted in Meagan Drillinger, "7 Steps to Breaking the 'Perfectionism, Procrastination, Paralysis' Cycle," Healthline, October 18, 2019. www.healthline.com.

When you're tired, hungry, or anxious, it's more difficult to get to work and concentrate on the task in front of you. Getting enough sleep and eating right play a role in your ability to do your best work. You need to avoid being pulled into a trap of trying to sacrifice sleep or your health to meet a deadline.

The challenges of getting enough sleep and eating right, as well as the brain's tendency to crave immediate rewards, might make you feel like you have a lot of excuses for not doing well in school or putting off your deadlines. But instead, these challenges mean that setting a schedule that you can stick to, getting enough sleep, and trying to eat right are more important than ever. The teen brain is adaptable and is strengthened by challenges and creative activities. You can learn to use strategies that give your brain the short-term rewards it craves while meeting your long-term goals. Developing good organizational habits now will pay off for the rest of your life.

Understanding Your Challenges

It's likely that you sometimes feel like you're more focused on the present, but at other times you're able to look toward the future. Maybe you have the discipline to practice playing the drums for half an hour a day or practice making free throws until you have made ten in a row because you know consistent practice will help you improve. At the same time, you might find it tough to avoid picking up your smartphone and scrolling through social media when you should be doing homework.

Your ability to focus and get stuff done will not only depend on what you are faced with but also how you feel about it and approach it. You might find large projects overwhelming or have difficulty keeping track of the many small assignments that you need to finish. For some people, doing it tomorrow is the answer to everything. If this is your style, just the thought of getting started

Perhaps you find yourself consistently misjudging how long something will take. When this happens time after time, you need to learn to build extra time into your schedule for work.

on a big assignment probably seems overwhelming or fills you with anxiety.

It might be exhilarating or exciting to put things off until the last minute. This feeling can be similar to an athlete's energy before a game or a performer's focus before going onstage. You might feel like you need this nervous energy before you can start working on a project. Some people do live their lives moving from deadline to deadline and feel a thrill when it all comes together in the end. You get the grade you wanted, or at least you pass the test, and that shows that you perform best when the pressure is on. That attitude, however, comes with a cost. "[Putting things off] strengthens the erroneous belief that work has to be unpleasant," says psychologist Adam Price. "Although the procrastinator becomes well practiced in avoidance, he never develops important skills such as planning, organization, thought development, and attention to detail."[10]

Perhaps you find yourself consistently misjudging how long something will take. You might think that an assignment will only take a few minutes, only to feel overwhelmed and anxious when it takes much longer than you expected. You might also decide to put off working on an assignment or project because you think it won't take long, only to find yourself working late into the night to get it done by the due date. When this happens time after time, you need to learn to build extra time into your schedule for work. Price compares it to buying things with a credit card. "It is easy and fun at first, but then you get the bill," he says. "And the interest is paid in feelings of dread, anxiety, helplessness, and self-hatred."[11]

It can also be tough to try to get stuff done because schoolwork, which may have once been easy for you, is now a challenge. An assignment might seem too hard, the teacher is going too fast, or there is too much homework. This can make you feel like a victim in a no-win situation. Price describes a student, Jeff,

> "Although the procrastinator becomes well practiced in avoidance, he never develops important skills such as planning, organization, thought development, and attention to detail."[10]
>
> —Psychologist Adam Price

who struggled with chemistry. He was smart, but he didn't seem interested in doing well in class. The real problem was that Jeff didn't know how to get work done. "Something his siblings and friends were able to do every night (sit down and do their homework) completely eluded him," Price explains. "This mystification only intensified his victimization."[12] Underneath Jeff's apathy was a feeling of helplessness and shame at not being able to get to work.

It's not easy to get through the frustration of a difficult class or try again after failing. You can, however, take steps, such as finding a tutor, working with a study buddy, and learning time management skills that help. Understanding that there are strategies that help you develop the ability to persevere and move forward will help you find the motivation to keep going the next time a difficult task arises.

CHAPTER TWO

Taking Control

Emma Elizabeth needs to arrive at school by 7:40 a.m., and even before she leaves, her entire day is mapped out. She goes to classes, has a break for lunch, and heads back to class until the school day ends. Once her final class of the day is over, she makes time for homework, chores, dinner, and a part-time job at the library. Although the schedule is just as full after school as the scheduled school day, she's on her own when it comes to planning out how to get everything done.

Teens have the freedom to use unstructured time as they please. Yet they still have obligations, like homework, chores, and perhaps work or volunteering commitments, that need to be met. Teens are in control of this unplanned time, but it can be easy to stumble when there's no clear road map for using it. "Teens usually have fairly structured schedules," notes psychotherapist Amy Morin, the editor in chief of the website Verywell Mind and author of *13 Things Strong Kids Do*. "Their school day and their after-school activities are planned out for them. Many of them don't learn how to manage their time wisely when they have downtime."[13] Having a plan for organizing your schedule, as well as your study space, can help you take control of your free time rather than wasting it.

Getting into a Routine

Making sure your day is organized, and that you have blocks of time for things you need to do, can start with a simple daily routine. In addition to school, your daily routine might include sports,

17

> "Once [a teen] gets into the routine of doing things in a certain order, he won't have to waste time thinking about what to do next."[14]
>
> —Psychotherapist Amy Morin

clubs, chores, or a part-time job in addition to homework. You might head home from school and feed the cats, clean their litter box, and start your homework. The next steps might include helping to get dinner ready, eating, finishing homework, and spending time doing something fun. Sports, clubs, volunteer work, or a part-time job might also be part of your routine, and it might be slightly different on different days of the week.

However it works out, getting into a routine can help ensure that you make time for your responsibilities and get into the habit of taking care of them. It can also take stress out of your day. You don't have to waste brainpower wondering where to go or what to do after the school day ends. "Once [a teen] gets into the routine of doing things in a certain order, he won't have to waste time thinking about what to do next,"[14] Morin says.

Making sure your day is organized can start with a simple daily routine. In addition to school, your daily routine might include sports, clubs, chores, or a part-time job in addition to homework.

Creating a Schedule

Your daily routine gives you a general idea of what's coming next, such as homework, sports, or an activity. To capture specific details, it's important to create written reminders of what needs to be done. Don't rely on your memory alone. "Let's face it," says teacher Rhonda Alamour. "There is too much going on in our daily lives to keep it all in our heads."[15]

To keep your tasks and deadlines front of mind, make a list of what you need to work on and use a calendar to write down due dates that are further away. To make your daily to-do list more effective, add details about what you will be working on. Don't just write down the name of a project or school subject, such as math or history. Write down what you plan to study or which part of a project you plan to complete. Rather than having "study" on your list, you could write "History, read pages 120 to 125. Take notes" or "Math, do problems 1 through 20."

> "Let's face it. There is too much going on in our daily lives to keep it all in our heads."[15]
>
> —Teacher Rhonda Alamour

It also helps to make a note to do things at a specific time. If it's your job to feed the dog, you're more likely to do it on time if you write "5:15—Feed Luna" on your list than if you just have "Feed dog" written down. If you need to be at school for a basketball game by 6 p.m., don't just put "game" on your schedule. Write down "Leave for game at 5:30 p.m."

You can use a written task list, daily planner, or organizing app to keep track of assignments or due dates. To stay on top of what she needs to do, Emma Elizabeth uses Google Calendar, a digital planner app, on her phone. "It's really nice to have a visual of everything that needs to be done," she says. "It's satisfying to see that I have everything done and I have checked it all off."[16]

You can also use your phone to cue you to do a task or head to an appointment. If you allow Google Calendar to send notifications, you'll see alerts for tasks and reminders, and you can mark them as completed. You can also receive audio signals. In

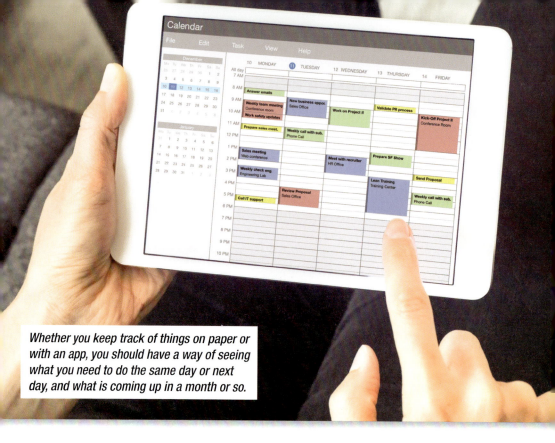

Whether you keep track of things on paper or with an app, you should have a way of seeing what you need to do the same day or next day, and what is coming up in a month or so.

addition, tasks and reminders can be set to repeat so that a music lesson that occurs each week at the same time only needs to be entered once and saved.

Although phone apps have the advantage of getting your attention with visual or sound notifications, there are some drawbacks, Alamour notes. "It's possible your phone will die and you'll lose access to all of your important information," she warns. "There are also times when you may not be able to use your phone, such as during class." This could keep you from entering a homework assignment into your app. She suggests carrying a daily planner and using the calendar section to keep track of big events, like tests, project due dates, or performances. The daily blocks can be used for your reminders and daily assignments and tasks. She also suggests including social events. "Seeing these fun events coming up later in the week will increase your motivation to get through your other less-interesting commitments,"[17] she says.

Although many strategies exist to keep track of assignments, extracurricular activities, and other commitments, they're only helpful if you actually use them. In addition, even with a task list or daily planner, a monthly calendar is essential for keeping track of due dates for larger projects. Whether you keep track of things on paper or with an app, you should have a way of seeing what you need to do today, tomorrow, and even in a month or two.

Clean Out Your Backpack

Many teens carry their daily planner, as well as a laptop or tablet, water bottle, folders, notebooks, and books, in a backpack. It's easy for papers to get lost in a crowded backpack, but folders can help. To avoid stuffing papers into your backpack and having them get crumpled and ignored, place papers in folders. Using a different colored folder for each class helps you easily find the one you need.

In addition, get into the habit of regularly cleaning out your backpack. You might be surprised at what you find in there. "So much gets lost in the black hole of a backpack," says Jane, who

Writing to Relieve Worry

When you have so much to do that it feels like your head is spinning and you're worried about how you'll get it all done, grab a pen and paper and start writing. Don't worry about what you say because this won't be read by anyone else. You can write freely about what comes to mind. Getting your thoughts and feelings on paper can relieve stress and help you work more efficiently.

Researcher Hans Schroder studied this by having students who were chronic worriers do an eight-minute writing exercise. Some wrote expressively, and others wrote a chronological timeline. Students who wrote expressively did better on a task, and a device measuring their brainwaves showed that they didn't have to think as hard about it. "Our findings show that if you get these worries out of your head through expressive writing, those cognitive resources are freed up to work toward the task you're completing and you become more efficient."

Quoted in Michigan State University, "For Worriers, Expressive Writing Cools Brain on Stressful Tasks," *MSU Today*, September 14, 2017. https://msutoday.msu.edu.

worked many years as a high school guidance counselor. "If you clean it out every night, it is maybe 10 minutes. Then you can work on homework."[18]

Optimize Your Space

A disorganized workspace strains your brain as well. You can set up your space in a way that gives you the best opportunity to accomplish your goals and complete assignments. Keeping your work area organized will help you work efficiently, lower your stress level, and have more time to do what you enjoy.

When you're trying to get stuff done, it helps to work in a space that's well organized. Keep the tools that will make you productive nearby. This may include a daily planner, list, or app for managing your schedule. If you use a laptop, figure out where you can plug it in and recharge so it doesn't die just as you're putting the final touches on your homework.

Also, make sure your work area is free of distractions so you can focus on your homework. For many people, this means that the area is quiet. If your home environment is chaotic and noisy, see if you can head to the library, or another place where you can focus, after school.

Using Time Management to Clean Up

If you find that a cluttered environment is distracting you, you can use some time management tips to quickly improve your work environment.

For a quick start, look for the easiest things you can do that will make a big difference. Maybe it's picking up all the dirty laundry and putting it in a basket, stacking the papers on your desk, or setting your charging devices in one spot. You could also begin with the spot that's bothering you the most. Is it the pile of clothes on your dresser? The mess on your desk? The jumble of shoes in the closet?

To make the task less overwhelming, set a timer for ten minutes, and see how much you can get done in this amount of time. To make it more enjoyable, turn on some music or a podcast. You could start in one corner of the room and move clockwise as you clean or break the room into sections and clean one area at a time. Even if you don't get the whole room cleaned, you'll have made an improvement. This can set the stage for a productive study session.

When you're done with your homework, clean up your space. It might be tempting to leave things messy, but cleaning things up allows you to clear your mind.

Working in an uncluttered workspace will also make it easier to concentrate on your homework. Clutter is distracting and makes it difficult to focus, notes psychologist Sherrie Bourg Carter. "Clutter bombards our minds with excessive stimuli (visual, olfactory, tactile), causing our senses to work overtime on stimuli that aren't necessary or important,"[19] she explains.

Your workspace should make you feel productive, energized, and creative. Like many students, Emerson, a high school junior, likes to do her homework on her bed. However, when she really needs to concentrate, she moves to the kitchen table. Sitting at a table or desk can help with focus because working on a laptop while lying on your bed strains your body. If you try to work in that position for a long time, you might start to feel achy and sore. You can't do your best work if your body isn't feeling right. You work most effectively when your body is ready to go.

When you're working at a computer, you sit at a desk or table with your feet flat on the floor. The laptop screen should be at eye level, so you're not hunched over. Sit up straight, and don't lean forward to look at the screen. If you make an effort to have the correct posture while doing your homework, you might be surprised that your assignments actually seem easier to do. That's because you're not fighting against your body, and more energy can be devoted to getting your work done.

When you're done with your homework, clean up your space. It might be tempting to leave things messy because you're only going to get everything out again tomorrow. However, cleaning things up allows you to clear your mind. "Not only will this give you a sense of closure when you leave but it will also make you feel good when you return to a nice, clean space,"[20] Carter says.

Experiment with Your Environment

Some people work best with as little noise as possible. Others find complete silence itself to be a distraction. They work better when there is a little bit of activity going on around them and may head to a coffee shop or café to study. Although a clean, well-organized environment can help with focus, you might find that a place other than your bedroom is where you do your best work. To see what works for you, test out a few different environments.

When you're studying at home, you can also try using your sense of smell to kick-start your motivation. Citrus scents encourage you to get going, notes interior designer Amy Farnum. After you're done studying, when you need to wind down and calm your brain, the smell of lavender helps you relax.

Navya Vasireddy, a high school sophomore, notes that a comfortable environment can include relaxing music, a candle, and perhaps a cup of hot chocolate or coffee. "Ambience has the potential to make or break one's concentration,"[21] she says.

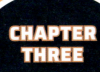

CHAPTER THREE

Do It Today

Autumn, age seventeen, knows that making it to appointments on time is her challenge. She often goes from school to her part-time job, and sometimes from there to watch her brother's hockey games. "It's kind of hard to manage,"[22] she admits, so she uses a reminder app on her phone to keep track of what's going on and when she must be somewhere.

Everyone is different, and so are the challenges to time management and tactics to keep things on track. Some people find it easy to plan and organize, but it's more of a struggle for others. Some look at their list of assignments or stare at a big project and don't know where to start, and others can't seem to focus on what they're supposed to be doing. Don't feel bad if you constantly feel like you're behind on your homework or always seem to be rushing to complete an assignment. Everyone faces these challenges, and the ability to get things done is something that develops and can improve over time. There likely will be days when it seems like there is no way you're going to finish an assignment because everything is working against you. Realizing that there are tactics that can work for you—and understanding where you have failed, tried again, and succeeded—can help you to find the tools it takes to get the work done well and on time.

Microsteps

When one of Emma Elizabeth's teachers gives students time to work on homework during class, she takes advantage of it. She has learned that doing work in class whenever possible makes her evenings less stressful. "I try to get as much done as I can during the school day," she says. "Otherwise, I have to finish it after work. I've learned that even if it's only ten minutes, at least I get a start on an assignment."[23] Emma Elizabeth's strategy for getting her homework done could be called "microproductivity." She uses small amounts of free time during the day to work toward the larger goal of finishing her daily assignments.

This system can be taken a step further when a task in front of you just seems too big. If you don't know where to begin, start by doing the smallest possible thing that will move the project forward. You might put a date on the top of your paper. Then add your name. Go ahead and write a title, and a first sentence.

Taking these small steps can get you started because the easier you make it to do something, the less willpower will be required

Sometimes teachers give students time to work on homework during class. Learn to use small amounts of free time during the day to work toward the larger goal of finishing your daily assignments.

to do it. This technique can be used to get going and gain momentum. Taking tiny steps allows you to make progress and enjoy the psychological reward of accomplishing a goal.

Breaking Things Down

The most challenging projects can be those with long-term deadlines. You might have a lab report that's not due for a few days or a paper that doesn't need to be turned in until the end of the month. Big projects take more incremental planning than shorter projects. There might be phases to the project, such as research, writing topic sentences, and drafting an outline for a big research project.

Breaking a big project into parts and scheduling time to work on a part each week, for example, is essential for completing the project on time. "If you're not sure how much time to give yourself for each task, you could talk to your teacher or ask a friend," recommends Louisa, a teacher and tutor. She also suggests leaving at least one day for editing your project. "Don't work up until the last minute because you will leave mistakes in the paper or project that can cost you,"[24] she said.

Avoiding the Planning Fallacy

When estimating how long you think something will take you to complete, don't be surprised if it actually ends up taking longer than expected. People tend to underestimate the amount of time it will take to finish a task, even when they know things have taken them longer in the past. In 1979, psychologists Daniel Kahneman and Amos Tversky called this the "planning fallacy." In 1994, social psychologist Roger Buehler and professor Dale Griffin conducted an experiment with college students that shows how this works. They asked the students to estimate the minimum and maximum amount of time it would take to write their senior theses. On average, students estimated it would take 33.9 days to finish their senior theses. Their estimated minimum time for completing it was 27.7 days, on average, and the maximum was 48.6 days.

Even if you make a specific plan to complete a large homework project, unexpected delays and interruptions are bound to occur. Be sure to make adjustments if you are getting off track.

> "When it comes to plans and predictions, people can know the past well and yet be doomed to repeat it."[25]
>
> —Psychologist Roger Buehler

The actual completion time turned out to be a week longer than their most pessimistic estimate: 55.5 days. "An intriguing aspect of the planning fallacy is that people simultaneously hold optimistic expectations concerning a specific future task along with more realistic beliefs concerning how long it has taken them to get things done in the past," Buehler says. "When it comes to plans and predictions, people can know the past well and yet be doomed to repeat it."[25]

Planning to Succeed

Falling into the planning fallacy could lead you to miss a deadline or need to work late into the night to finish a project on time. To avoid that, break your project into small, specific parts, and estimate how long each of these components will take. Estimate how long it took you to write one section of your lab report or one page of an essay. "When we do this, our predicted times to completion are more accurate,"[26] notes psychology teacher Sue Frantz.

In addition, make a specific plan for finishing the project. Decide not only when you will work on it, but where you are going to work on each specific part. "When we decide when and where we are going to do these subtasks, we are more likely to complete them in the time predicted,"[27] Frantz says.

As you work on the project, be aware of how closely your progress matches your estimates. Unexpected delays and interruptions are bound to occur. Make adjustments if you're getting off track. You might need to read more pages per day or spend two days writing an outline rather than one. Staying on top of your schedule can help you complete the project on time without rushing to finish.

Deciding on Priorities

When you have a big project coming due but are obligated to complete other homework assignments, it can be difficult to make the long-term project a priority. A big project might not be

Not Sure How Long This Should Take? Ask Someone

When you're tackling a new project, it can be difficult to determine how long it will take you. Taking the step of talking to others can help you avoid making the mistake of looking at only the "insider view." The insider view focuses only on the tasks you need to accomplish rather than looking at the big picture to see what roadblocks you might face. "We very rarely take the time to research similar projects, interview experts, and learn from other people how they tackled the problem, what went wrong and what they wish they knew at the time," explains researcher Anne-Laure Le Cunff, founder of Ness Labs.

To avoid this, talk to others who have done a similar project. This can give you an outside view that considers the obstacles you may face, not only what you need to do. "If you're a student, talk to senior students; if you're a product manager, email someone at another startup; if you're writing a book, join a network of writers," Le Cunff advises. "Ask questions before you start outlining your plan."

Anne-Laure Le Cunff, "The Planning Fallacy: Why We Underestimate How Long a Task Will Take," Ness Labs, April 3, 2023. https://nesslabs.com.

due for weeks, and it may not seem important to work on it now. The consequences of failing to complete it are far away, and other assignments are more urgent.

Teacher and tutor Louisa recommends working on the long-term project first because planning to work on it last might mean you don't work on it at all. "You may run out of time in the evening or just run out of energy," she notes. "But putting it first on the list ensures that the steps actually get done—that way you won't be scrambling the night before it's due."[28]

The Ivy Lee Method

If you're trying to decide what to do first, one way to organize your tasks is to use the Ivy Lee method. Ivy Lee was a productivity expert who developed a system for helping people make the best use of their time. Lee's system stems from 1918, when Charles M. Schwab, the president of the Bethlehem Steel Corporation,

Ivy Lee (pictured) was a productivity expert who developed a system for helping people make the best use of their time. The system involves creating a list of six important things to do for the following day.

hired him to improve productivity at his company. Schwab was so impressed with the results of Lee's method that he paid him $25,000, which would be equal to more than $400,000 today.

The Ivy Lee system involves creating a list of six things to do tomorrow. The tasks are organized from most important to least important. The list is tackled from top to bottom. The next task cannot be started until the one before it has been completed. At the end of the day, anything that is unfinished is moved to the list for the next day.

The advantage of this method is that it is simple to use and allows you to easily identify your priorities. It forces you to decide what is most important and focus your energy on it. "I do think there is something magical about imposing limits upon yourself. I find that the single best thing to do when you have too many ideas (or when you're overwhelmed by everything you need to get done) is to prune your ideas and trim away everything that isn't absolutely necessary," insists James Clear, the author of *Atomic Habits*. "Basically, if you commit to nothing, you'll be distracted by everything."[29]

> "If you commit to nothing, you'll be distracted by everything."[29]
>
> —Author James Clear

Clearly, we may have more than six things we need to do, but these tasks can also be added to the list. But Lee's idea of keeping the list short has also been a proven winner—if your list becomes too long there can be a feeling of defeat that you can never get it all done. A shorter list of immediate priorities can help you decide what urgently needs your focus. You could create a list of six priorities on Friday so you aren't left wondering where to start on Saturday with your weekend homework assignments. You can jump right into your work without wasting time trying to decide what to do first.

Eat That Frog

There is a saying, which some credit to Mark Twain, that if you eat a frog first thing in the morning, nothing worse will happen to you the rest of the day. In other words, do the hardest thing first. As far

Working Toward Long-Term Goals

On any given day there are short-term goals to meet, such as finishing assignments or making it to basketball practice on time. During the school year, you likely have larger goals as well. These might not relate directly to your classwork but could make an important impact on your future. Maybe you want to submit college applications or exercise more. To meet these larger goals, set smaller time-bound goals that will help you get there.

If you want to apply to three colleges by December, set aside time each Saturday to work on this. On one Saturday, look into the admissions process for one college and make a list of what's needed. Then make a schedule for gathering everything on that list.

If you want to exercise more, look into options that interest you. Maybe there's a yoga class that meets for an hour on Monday, Wednesday, and Friday, or perhaps you want to run with a friend on Tuesdays and Thursdays. Decide on a specific activity and time and make it part of your schedule.

Using smaller, attainable goals and assigning a time frame to them will help you reach a long-term goal.

---

as productivity is concerned, tackling your most unpleasant task first can make everything else seem easy.

This task could be the one you dislike the most or the one you find most challenging. It could be something you fear you won't do well, or something new you are afraid to try.

You could try this tip on a Saturday, or another day when school is not in session, and get that tough task out of the way early in the day. Most people are sharpest in the morning, and their focus is best at that time of day. In addition, getting your homework out of the way allows you to be guilt-free when you move on to things you'd rather be doing with your time.

This technique does not have to be used only on nonschool days, however. You can also use this tip when you're starting an after-school homework session. Begin with the subject you like the least. This allows you to get it out of the way and provides a sense of relief once it's done.

Other chores and obligations can be handled the same way. If you need to talk to a teacher about a bad grade, schedule some time before class to discuss it. That way, you won't have to dread the meeting for the whole day.

Create Your Own System

Many other time management schemes exist, and it can be fun to play around with how others get things done and try them for yourself. Finding the approach that works best for you will likely be a blend of ideas. "Different systems work for different people," explains productivity expert Laura Vanderkam. "If a system generally works, people are going to need to modify it in some way, shape or form. If you go into the productivity literature with that in mind, rather than attempting to find the one gospel truth, you will be a lot happier and a lot less frustrated when something doesn't work for you. Because nothing will work perfectly for everyone."[30]

CHAPTER FOUR

Dealing with Distraction

You're ready to start a set of math problems when your cell phone buzzes. You pick it up, start scrolling through social media, and before you know it twenty minutes have gone by. You set down your phone and start again when you get a text. You answer it and return to your homework. Then you smell something. Your brother just took a pizza out of the oven. Do you want a slice or two? Before you know it, distractions have kept you from getting anything done.

It's great to have a detailed plan for getting stuff done, but how do you stick to it? It's a challenge everyone struggles with. A study from the Institute of Education Sciences found that students spend a third of their homework time being distracted from it. Over a year, this adds up to 204 hours of wasted time.

Distractions abound, from social media notifications to texts from friends to interruptions from family members. To avoid distractions, you need to work in a place where you can concentrate. Then you need to find a way to focus and avoid being pulled away from the task at hand.

Why Your Brain Loves Your Smartphone

Like 95 percent of teens, Autumn has a smartphone. Although it's incredibly useful, it's also her biggest distraction. She's well aware of this and uses a screen-time counter to help her limit how much she uses it. "I like to keep my daily average somewhere below three hours," she says. "At the end of the week, I know if my average is above that I'm spending a little too much time on my phone."[31]

Smartphones are a great homework tool when they help you find the information you need, but they can also hurt your productivity. It's extremely difficult to ignore texts from friends and social media notifications. A phone's buzz or ping can quickly pull you away from the homework you should be focusing on. "Because our brains are evolutionarily designed to pay attention to novelty, these alerts are almost impossible to ignore," explains writer Dana G. Smith. "And if you try to, you'll likely find your anxiety mounting."[32]

Researchers tested the effect of a smartphone's buzz in an experiment in which participants could hear the buzz of their phones but could not pick them up to see the notifications. Those in the experiment had been told that their smartphones would interfere with research equipment. When researchers texted the participants' phones, monitors on the participants' skin recorded their reaction and showed that they were affected by the sound. "They felt like they needed to answer that text or at least see who it was from, and they couldn't," explains psychology professor Larry Rosen, a coauthor on the study. "And that gave them anxiety."[33]

Social media apps are designed to make us want to use them as often as possible. They provide a constant flow of new information, and seeing people like and react to your posts makes you feel good. They also take advantage of the pull of random rewards. When something happens on a regular schedule, it becomes expected and can lose its luster. Random events are more enticing because they have the element of surprise. By bringing good feelings on a random schedule, social media encourages you to keep going back to it. You never know when you're going to get a text from a friend or when one of your posts will go viral.

Even when you pick up your smartphone for just a moment, it hurts your productivity. Minor disruptions like checking a text message cause you to stop focusing on what you're doing. Your

Smartphones are a great homework tool when they help you find the information you need, but they can also hurt your productivity. It's difficult to ignore texts from friends and social media notifications.

brain needs to switch to a different task, and this is more tiring than simply concentrating on what needs to be done. "If you're constantly being interrupted, it's going to take you a long time to get your work done,"[34] writer Rose Leadem notes.

The Myth of Multitasking

If you're watching a video for class while also texting with a friend, checking social media, or working on another homework assignment, you might congratulate yourself on being able to do so many things at the same time. But when you multitask, your mind is actually switching its attention from one thing to another very quickly. This is tiring and less effective than concentrating on one thing at a time. "People usually think that they're getting more done by multitasking, but in reality, going back and forth from task to task isn't beneficial,"[35] says Leadem.

Studies show that you are up to 40 percent less productive when you try to multitask, even when switching to something else takes only a fraction of a second. If you try to multitask, your brain can get tired. This can lead to more mistakes being made and may hurt your creativity. "You can only be thinking about one thing at a time," explains behavioral scientist Susan Weinschenk. "So you can be talking or you can be reading. You can be reading or you can be typing. You can be listening or you can be reading. One thing at a time." Even though it might seem like you can watch a video and do homework at the same time, you're not giving either task your full concentration. "We fool ourselves," Weinschenk says. "We are pretty good at switching back and forth quickly, so we THINK we are actually multitasking, but in reality we are not."[36]

We can do a physical task we have done many times before while we also do a mental task. You can talk and walk at the same time, for example. However, even this has limits. When we talk on a cell phone, we are not as aware of our surroundings as we usually are. Ira E. Hyman Jr., a researcher at Western Washington University, led a 2009 study that showed this. Hyman had a student put on a purple-and-yellow clown suit and pedal a unicycle around the campus square for an hour. Researchers then asked people who had walked across the square if they had seen the unicycling clown. Only 25 percent of people using a cell phone noticed the clown, whereas 71 percent of those walking with a friend recalled seeing the clown. In addition, 61 percent of those listening to music and 51 percent of people walking alone remembered the clown. "It shows that even during as simple a task as walking, performance drops off when talking on the cellphone,"[37] Hyman observed.

> "We are pretty good at switching back and forth quickly, so we THINK we are actually multitasking, but in reality we are not."[36]
>
> —Behavioral scientist Susan Weinschenk

Resisting Distractions

To change your multitasking behavior, accept that you need to get rid of the distractions that are taking your focus off what you should be working on. The buzz of social media notifications may make you feel good, but checking social media while you're studying will make your study session less effective.

At Emma Elizabeth's high school, some teachers require students to put their phones in a "phone pocket" before class. Your school might have a similar rule or call it "phone jail." At Emma Elizabeth's school, the pockets, which are the size of a phone, are at the front of the classroom. Each student is assigned a phone pocket and their phones stay in the pockets during class. "It's definitely a little hard; during free time you want to check it and see if you have any texts, but I've been able to get used to it,"[38] she says.

At home, you can create your own version of a phone pocket to get rid of social media distractions while you do your homework. It's easier to forget about your phone if you can't hear it buzzing or dinging. You can turn off the volume, place the phone in a drawer, or turn it off and set it on the other side of the room. For some people, simply having the phone in the room with them is a distraction. If this is you, put your phone in another room while you're studying. When you put a barrier between yourself and the distraction, the extra effort it takes to get to it will help you break the habit of reaching for it every time you get bored or stuck on a problem.

Want to Be Left Alone?

When you need to focus, you don't want to be bothered. If you're in the library or a study hall and don't want others to bother you, you can use your headphones to help you focus. You don't need to listen to music or a podcast. Just have your headphones in your ears. It's a signal to others that you are in your own zone and don't want to be disturbed. People are less likely to try and talk to you if they see you have your headphones in.

It is important to get rid of social media and other smartphone distractions when doing homework. Turning off your phone or putting it in another room is a good idea.

Another option is to delete social media apps from your phone altogether, use distraction blocker apps, or use apps that encourage you to set your phone aside for a certain amount of time. The apps can help you avoid the distraction of your phone by limiting your access to websites after a certain time limit or giving you more stats about your usage.

If you find it tough to think about going phone-free, break your study session into blocks of time. For one block of time, get rid of all electronic distractions by setting your phone aside, turning down the volume, or getting rid of notifications. If you can, close the door to your room or go to a place where you can be alone to keep other distractions away as well. Work only on your task for that block of time. "You will be amazed at how much you will accomplish and how energized it makes you feel,"[39] states Weinschenk.

Using a Tomato Timer

You can also train yourself to focus for longer periods of time by concentrating on your project for a limited amount of time. One way to do this is with a method named after a tomato-shaped timer. The Pomodoro Technique was invented by Francesco Cirillo, who was a student in Rome during the late 1980s. Cirillo used a timer shaped like a tomato to time his study sessions, and his study method became known as the Pomodoro Technique because *pomodoro* is the Italian word for "tomato."

To use this method, set any timer for twenty-five minutes and focus on your project during that time. Then take a five-minute break. After four of these twenty-minute periods, you can take a longer break of 20 to 30 minutes. You don't need to use all four study periods, but you can use the general idea of focusing for a set amount of time and then taking a brief break to get through a study session of any length.

The technique also gives you a deadline; you may want to get something done before the timer goes off. This can motivate you to stay focused on your work. In addition, because it helps you understand how much you can get done in a certain amount of time,

The Cost of Multitasking

If you send texts or check social media while doing homework or when you're in class, this brief distraction could have a bigger impact than you might realize. A study by researchers at the University of Connecticut looked at the multitasking habits of more than 350 college students. They were asked to describe how often they multitasked in class and while doing homework and report their grade point average, how much time they spent preparing for class, and how good they thought they were at multitasking.

The study found that students who multitasked while doing homework had to study longer. Those who multitasked during class had lower grades on average than students who multitasked less often. Texting was the multitasking distraction students reported most often, followed by social media, checking email, and browsing the internet. "People often put their phones away when they are meeting with friends or having dinner," noted researcher Saraswati Bellur. "Those are mindful, conscious decisions. It would be nice if students brought that same kind of mindfulness to class."

Colin Poitras, "Multitasking Increases Study Time, Lowers Grades," UConn Today, July 23, 2015. https://today.uconn.edu.

consistently using the Pomodoro Technique can help you understand how long the entire project will take you. This can help you make sure you set aside enough time to get it done.

> "If you work for 5 or 10 minutes, or even 1 minute, you are making progress."[40]
>
> —Productivity coach Paula Rizzo

Productivity coach Paula Rizzo uses this method and notes that it can be challenging to concentrate on one thing for this amount of time at first. "If it's tough for you to concentrate for 25 minutes at first, it's fine to begin with shorter amounts of time," she says. "If you work for 5 or 10 minutes, or even 1 minute, you are making progress."[40]

When It Comes to Managing Your Smartphone, It's Your Call

Restricting your phone use is difficult because it is mostly self-imposed. A study published in *Education Sciences* found that two-thirds of families didn't have restrictions on phone use during homework. Of those that did have rules, less than a third of students followed them. Avoiding smartphone distraction is critical to getting stuff done, but the motivation to do that needs to come from within.

When you respond to social media or text message notifications on your phone, you are reacting rather than acting. The phone has taken control of your time. To get stuff done, you need to be the one in charge. You can use apps, phone jail, and other distraction-blocking techniques to gradually break your smartphone habit. Little by little, you can keep social media notifications and text messages from taking control of your attention and breaking your focus.

Putting limits on your social media usage involves discipline, and it can take time to break the smartphone habit and build up your ability to concentrate on a task. Every time you make the effort to stay focused and avoid distractions, you're moving toward your goal of completing your task. As you get better at it, you will find it easier to focus and get stuff done.

Recharging

Although staying focused on your work is important, taking a brief break during a longer study session can help you do your best work. Your brain and body benefit when you pause for a short time. "We can't expect to lift weights nonstop all day, and we can't expect to use sustained focus and attention for extended periods of time, either,"[41] says Gloria Mark, a professor and the author of *Attention Span: A Groundbreaking Way to Restore Balance, Happiness and Productivity*.

A short break can revive your brain and help you solve a tough problem. The part of the brain that is creative is the prefrontal cortex. It works on one thing at a time. This part of your brain also needs quiet time to process information. If you're

While staying focused on your work is important, taking a brief break during a longer study session can help you do your best work. Your brain and body benefit when you pause for a short time.

working on a project that involves creativity, such as writing an essay or thinking of ideas for a term paper, a short daydreaming break can help your brain generate new ideas. "Mind-wandering facilitates the kind of solution that just comes to you, as in a lightbulb moment,"[42] says researcher Julie Kam of the University of Calgary.

During this break, you could listen to music, look out the window and daydream, or exercise. One of the best ways to give your brain a break is to take a walk outside. Nature and physical activity can boost creativity and reduce stress. By letting your mind wander a bit, you're giving it a chance to work differently. "The default mode network can actually retrieve details from the nooks and crannies in your brain's memories that the logical brain cannot retrieve," explains psychiatrist Srini Pillay, "which is why sometimes people say they have their best ideas in the shower."[42]

CHAPTER FIVE

Overcoming Procrastination

It might seem like a great idea to wait until the last minute to finish a math assignment or work on a lab report. After all, you have plenty of time. Organizing your sock drawer, cleaning out your backpack, putting books on your bookshelf in alphabetical order, scrolling through social media, or even making sure all your pens work may seem like a much better use of your time right now.

Psychology professor Fuschia Sirois of Durham University tells of one student who hated cleaning—except when he had a big paper or exam coming up. "Instead of doing studying, he was running around getting the house perfectly clean," she says. "You see this a lot. It's not like procrastinators are sitting around lazy, they're doing other things. It's just not that thing that they should be doing right now that's looming and important and will have negative consequences if they don't get it done."[43]

Intentional Avoidance

Procrastinators intentionally avoid a necessary task. They choose not to work on something that could be challenging, boring, difficult, frustrating, or time-consuming. "Procrastination is not waiting and it is more than delaying," says psychology professor Joseph Ferrari. "It is a decision to not act."[44]

In some ways, this makes no sense. Avoiding a task, assignment, or responsibility doesn't make it go away, it only makes it harder to get it done on time. Why do we procrastinate when we know it will turn out badly? It has a lot to do with the way our brain works.

We are primed to focus on the now. When something can be done at any time, we are less motivated to do it because we won't be rewarded immediately. Our brains have taught us to focus on the present, and at present it's much more pleasurable to avoid working on something we'd rather not do. "We really weren't designed to think ahead into the further future because we needed to focus on providing for ourselves in the here and now,"[45] says psychologist Hal Hershfield, a professor at the University of California, Los Angeles.

> "We really weren't designed to think ahead into the further future because we needed to focus on providing for ourselves in the here and now."[45]
>
> —Psychologist Hal Hershfield

To find out how we look at ourselves in the future, Hershfield led a study that used images of the brain. He found that we use the same part of the brain to think about ourselves in the future as we do when we think of other people. In effect, when we look at ourselves in the future, it is as if we are looking at another person. When we procrastinate, we don't want to burden ourselves with doing a task now, so we give it to someone else—our future self. "We're trying to make ourselves feel good when we procrastinate," explains psychology professor Tim Pychyl, the author of *Solving the Procrastination Puzzle*. "Our present self wins and future self loses."[46]

Why Procrastination Feels Good

The rough part about procrastinating is that it really does feel good in the moment. You're not imagining this. Thinking about doing something unpleasant brings up negative emotions. When we avoid this task, our brain rewards us for procrastinating by making those emotions disappear and providing a sense of relief. "Procrastination is an emotion regulation problem, not a time management problem,"[47] Pychyl notes.

Procrastinators intentionally avoid doing a necessary task. Instead of studying for a final exam, for example, they do household chores instead.

If you haven't had a lot of practice overcoming negative emotions, you might find that coping with a challenging task is something you don't feel you can do right now. Avoiding it is better than trying to work through the stress, anxiety, frustration, or boredom you are afraid it will bring. "If it's something unpleasant and we can't quite work through those feelings, procrastination becomes a way to solve that, at least in the short run,"[48] Sirois says.

The Problem with Procrastination

The problem with failing to work through those feelings is that procrastination can easily become a habit. Procrastination rewards us with a good feeling, and this reinforces our desire to do it again the next time a difficult task arises.

These good feelings are only temporary, however. You will eventually need to get the task done, and if you keep procrastinating, it only becomes more difficult to move past those negative feelings and begin to move toward our goal. Roadblocks that might have been minor if you had started early, like a broken printer, an illness, or drama with friends that needs to be sorted out, take on added significance and might derail your ability to get something done. "If you're a student and you're procrastinating on your academic work, then it's likely you're not going to do as well performance-wise," Sirois states. "You're going to hand in things late or you're not going to do your best work. And the research bears this out. Students who chronically procrastinate tend to have poorer performance in terms of their grades."[49]

Chronic Procrastination

Everyone puts things off from time to time; between 80 and 95 percent of college students procrastinate at least once or more, Sirois notes. If you don't learn to manage the emotions that come with doing something difficult, challenging, or unpleasant, you risk becoming a chronic procrastinator—like 15 to 25 percent of working adults.

Sirois sees this ultimately affecting your ability to live up to your full potential and enjoy your life. "The people that I've spoken

The Two-Minute Rule

When you find it tough to get started on a project, giving yourself the option of working on something for only a few minutes could be the key to getting down to work.

Writer Joshua Becker says the two-minute rule always works for him. When he finds himself procrastinating, he tells himself he will just work on a project for two minutes. Then he commits to doing two minutes of work. Focusing on this specific time commitment makes even an unpleasant task seem manageable. "For me, getting started is the greatest battle," he says. "Once I begin the task, I almost end up spending more than the two minutes—usually completing the entire task or a significant portion of it."

Joshua Becker, "The Simple Tool I Use to Overcome Procrastination," Becoming Minimalist. www.becomingminimalist.com.

to who really struggle with procrastination, they are in a bad way," she says. "They have career issues, health issues, they're not fulfilling their dreams, they're not reaching their goals."[50]

Sirois's research has also found that chronic procrastination may affect mental and physical health. It's associated with higher rates of depression, anxiety, and stress and can also weaken the immune system. This makes a person more likely to catch a cold or the flu. Chronic procrastinators may put off doing things that could help their health, such as exercising or changing their diets. "If you're changing your diet, something that can be unpleasant, you have to give up some foods that you really enjoy, getting off the couch and away from the screen and getting out and doing physical exercise, if you're not used to it, that can be

Good feelings that come from procrastination are only temporary. If you keep procrastinating it only becomes more difficult to move past the negative feelings that come from facing a challenging task.

unpleasant to start, too," Sirois says. "It's not surprising that we find that people who chronically procrastinate also tend to put off engaging in those health promoting behaviors that would really help their health overall."[51]

Getting Started

Although chronic procrastination is a problem, it can be overcome. With practice, you can learn to manage the negative emotions that are causing you to avoid a task. Ask yourself what those emotions and feelings are and what benefit there is to feeling them. Then, even though those feelings are still there, take a step toward beginning your project. "If I'm feeling afraid, I can feel afraid and still take this next step,"[52] comments life coach Sarah Hoover.

Pychyl suggests taking the smallest action possible. Succeeding at that will give you the confidence to keep going. "Research has shown us that when you make progress, even a little bit on a goal, it fuels your wellbeing," he says. "Even if you just take the tiniest of steps, you'll help yourself get started and then you're on your way."[53]

Daniel Wong, who coaches teens on academic motivation, suggests putting your homework on your desk, so it's there in front of you, and writing about the task that's making you procrastinate. "You might be surprised to discover that simply by writing down the specific task you're putting off, the situation will feel more manageable,"[54] he says.

Finding something meaningful or enjoyable in a task can also help you avoid procrastinating and get down to work. If you find something pleasant about an assignment, you're more likely to actually work on it. You can start with the easiest part or look for an interesting article that relates to your research topic. You can also plan to reward yourself with some social media scrolling or watching your favorite show when you're finished. Doing this lets you approach the work in a way that makes your brain decide that working on this task right now is better than procrastinating.

Being Mindful

Mindfulness can help to control the emotions that keep you from doing a task. If you are worried about a task, take some deep breaths or try tensing and then relaxing your muscles. Be aware of your emotions, but do not judge them. Acknowledge that the feelings are there, but don't let them get the best of you. "For example, you could say, 'I'm really anxious about this report.' And then look for the reasons for those emotions," suggests psychology professor Tim Pychyl. "Maybe you don't want to disappoint. That makes sense. Your emotions are trying to teach you something. But you don't need to freak out. My favorite saying is, 'I can have anxiety. I don't need to be my anxiety.'"

Learning more about mindfulness, and practicing it, can help you regulate your emotions, which may help you procrastinate less. A study from the University of Pittsburgh showed that in individuals who practiced mindfulness for eight weeks, the amygdala, the part of the brain associated with emotion and fear, became smaller, and there were changes to the connections with the prefrontal cortex, the part of the brain associated with planning and decision-making.

Quoted in Stephanie Vozza, "This Is What Happens to Your Brain When You Procrastinate," *Fast Company*, September 22, 2021. www.fastcompany.com.

Share Your Goal

Another tactic is to let others know what you are working on and when you expect to have it done. When you are aware that others know you should be working on something, that can motivate you to stick to your task. "We have a little extra motivation to work when we publicly make a commitment to someone else,"[55] explains Will Canu, a psychology professor at Appalachian State University.

You could let a classmate or family member know that you are going to write one paragraph of an essay or do three math problems by a certain time. They could tell you about something they're working on. Then you can check in on each other and see if you've both met your goals.

Don't Be Too Hard on Yourself

If you find yourself procrastinating or do fail to meet a goal or miss a deadline, don't be too hard on yourself. Being compassionate with yourself can help support your motivation for moving forward productively. According to Pychyl's studies, when people forgive themselves for procrastinating, they procrastinate less the next time they face that task. "It's important for people to recognize that you're going to screw up," he says. "You're going to make mistakes, and you're going to procrastinate some days when you don't want to work. You have to have some self-compassion. Forgive yourself so you'll try again."[56]

> "You have to have some self-compassion. Forgive yourself so you'll want to try again."[56]
>
> —Psychology professor Tim Pychyl

A good technique is to let others know what you plan to accomplish. You could let a family member know that you are going to write one page of an essay or complete math problems by a certain time.

Sometimes it is difficult to begin a project because you expect to do your best work right away. If you simply can't get started because your inner critic keeps telling you your work isn't good enough, just get to work without judging the quality. This keeps self-doubt from holding you back. "So often, procrastination is really about fear of imperfection or outright failure," comments Phyllis Korkki, the author of *The Big Thing*, a book about overcoming procrastination. "That's why we tend to offload a demanding task to our future self—a self that will magically be more well-equipped than our present self to get something done. Working hard in the present means shedding an idealized image of your final product. You'll have time later to shine and buff your work. For now, just get going."[57]

SOURCE NOTES

Introduction: Managing It All

1. Emerson, interview with the author, February 17, 2023.
2. Quoted in Dana G. Smith, "How to Focus Like It's 1990," *New York Times,* January 9, 2023. www.nytimes.com.
3. Quoted in Kim Mills, "Why Our Attention Spans Are Shrinking, with Gloria Mark, PhD," *Speaking of Psychology* (podcast), Episode 225, American Psychological Association, February 2023. www.apa.org.

Chapter One: Why Is It Tough to Get Stuff Done?

4. Autumn, interview with the author, March 5, 2023.
5. Quoted in Amy Brooks, "70% of High Schoolers Aren't Getting Enough Sleep," *Healthier, Happy Lives Blog,* Stanford Medicine, August 21, 2019. https://healthier.stanfordchildrens.org.
6. Quoted in Ruthann Richter, "Among Teens, Sleep Deprivation an Epidemic," Stanford Medicine, October 8, 2015. https://med.stanford.edu.
7. Emerson, interview.
8. Kamogelo, "Toxic Productivity," *Voices of Youth* (blog), January 1, 2020. www.voicesofyouth.org.
9. Kamogelo, "Toxic Productivity."
10. Adam Price, "4 Reasons Why Teens Can't Stop Procrastinating," *Procrastination* (blog), *Psychology Today,* April 17, 2018. www.psychologytoday.com.
11. Price, "4 Reasons Why Teens Can't Stop Procrastinating."
12. Price, "4 Reasons Why Teens Can't Stop Procrastinating."

Chapter Two: Taking Control

13. Amy Morin, "How to Teach Time Management Skills to Teens," *Verywell Family,* November 8, 2019. www.verywellfamily.com.
14. Morin, "How to Teach Time Management Skills to Teens."
15. Rhonda Alamour, "How to Be More Organized in High School: The Student's Guide," *Admissions Strategist* (blog), Transizion, October 27, 2022. www.transizion.com.
16. Emma Elizabeth, interview with the author, March 27, 2023.
17. Alamour, "How to Be More Organized in High School."
18. Jane, interview with the author, March 24, 2023.

19. Sherrie Bourg Carter, "Why Mess Causes Stress: 8 Reasons, 8 Remedies," *Stress* (blog), *Psychology Today,* March 14, 2012. www.psychologytoday.com.
20. Carter, "Why Mess Causes Stress."
21. Navya Vasireddy, "5 Effective Tips to Increase Productivity and Decrease Stress," *Teen Magazine,* March 15, 2023. www.theteenmagazine.com.

Chapter Three: Do It Today

22. Autumn, interview.
23. Emma Elizabeth, interview.
24. Louisa, "How to Actually Complete Your Long-Term Project," LP Tutoring. https://lptutoring.com.
25. Roger Buehler, "The Planning Fallacy: An Inside View," *Society for Personality and Social Psychology* (blog), May 30, 2019. https://spsp.org.
26. Sue Frantz, "Helping Students Overcome the Planning Fallacy," Macmillan Learning, April 14, 2021. https://community.macmillanlearning.com.
27. Frantz, "Helping Students Overcome the Planning Fallacy."
28. Louisa, "How to Actually Complete Your Long-Term Project."
29. James Clear, "The Ivy Lee Method: The Daily Routine Experts Recommend for Peak Productivity," James Clear. https://jamesclear.com.
30. Quoted in Angela Haupt, "Set a Tomato Timer? Eat a Frog? Be Like Ike? Comparing 5 Common Productivity Systems," *Washington Post,* August 2, 2021. www.washingtonpost.com.

Chapter Four: Dealing with Distraction

31. Autumn, interview.
32. Smith, "How to Focus Like It's 1990."
33. Quoted in Smith, "How to Focus Like It's 1990."
34. Leadem, "17 Tricks to Get More Done During the Work Day," *Entrepreneur,* September 28, 2016. www.entrepreneur.com.
35. Leadem, "17 Tricks to Get More Done During the Work Day."
36. Susan Weinschenk, "The True Cost of Multi-Tasking," *Career* (blog), *Psychology Today,* September 12, 2012. www.psychologytoday.com.
37. Quoted in Tara Parker-Pope, "What Clown on a Unicycle? Studying Cellphone Distraction," *Well* (blog), *New York Times,* October 22, 2009. https://archive.nytimes.com.
38. Emma Elizabeth, interview.
39. Weinschenk, "The True Cost of Multi-Tasking."

40. Quoted in Jenny Powers, "An Emmy Award–Winning TV Producer and Productivity Coach Shares How Leaders Can Better Manage Their Time," *Insider,* March 5, 2021. www.businessinsider.com.
41. Quoted in A.C. Shilton, "How to Tell If Your Brain Needs a Break," *New York Times,* February 3, 2023. www.nytimes.com.
42. Quoted in Jill Suttie, "Focus Is Important to Productivity. But It's Daydreaming That Makes Us Happy," *Washington Post,* August 2, 2021. www.washingtonpost.com.

Chapter Five: Overcoming Procrastination

43. Quoted in Kim Mills, "Why We Procrastinate and What to Do About It, with Fuschia Sirois, PhD," *Speaking of Psychology* (podcast), Episode 210, American Psychological Association, October 2022. www.apa.org.
44. Quoted in American Psychological Association, "Psychology of Procrastination: Why People Put Off Important Tasks Until the Last Minute," 2010. www.apa.org.
45. Quoted in Charlotte Lieberman, "Why You Procrastinate (It Has Nothing to Do with Self-Control)," *New York Times,* March 25, 2019. www.nytimes.com.
46. Quoted in Cey'Na Smith, "Three Tips to Help You Fight Procrastination," *Vox,* September 6, 2021. www.voxmagazine.com.
47. Quoted in Lieberman, "Why You Procrastinate."
48. Quoted in Mills, "Why We Procrastinate and What to Do About It, with Fuschia Sirois, PhD."
49. Quoted in Mills, "Why We Procrastinate and What to Do About It, with Fuschia Sirois, PhD."
50. Quoted in Mills, "Why We Procrastinate and What to Do About It, with Fuschia Sirois, PhD."
51. Quoted in Mills, "Why We Procrastinate and What to Do About It, with Fuschia Sirois, PhD."
52. Quoted in Smith, "Three Tips to Help You Fight Procrastination."
53. Quoted in Stephanie Vozza, "This Is What Happens to Your Brain When You Procrastinate," *Fast Company*, September 22, 2021. www.fastcompany.com.
54. Daniel Wong, "30 Tips to Stop Procrastinating and Find Motivation to Do Homework," Daniel Wong, January 24, 2023. www.daniel-wong.com.
55. Quoted in Kelsey Ables, "'Body Doubling,' an ADHD Productivity Tool, Is Flourishing Online," *Washington Post,* June 1, 2022. www.washingtonpost.com.
56. Quoted in Smith, "Three Tips to Help You Fight Procrastination."
57. Phyllis Korkki, "How to Be More Productive," *New York Times,* October 13, 2022. www.nytimes.com.

FOR FURTHER RESEARCH

Books

David Allen, Mike Williams, and Mark Wallace, *Getting Things Done for Teens: Take Control of Your Life in a Distracting World.* New York: Penguin, 2018.

Chris Bailey, *How to Calm Your Mind.* New York: Viking, 2022.

Lara Honos-Webb, *6 Super Skills for Executive Functioning: Tools to Help Teens Improve Focus, Stay Organized & Reach Their Goals.* Oakland, CA: Instant Help, 2020.

Barbara Oakley, Terrence Sejnowski, and Alistair McConville, *Learning How to Learn: How to Succeed in School Without Spending All Your Time Studying.* New York: TarcherPerigee, 2018.

Internet Sources

Angela Haupt, "Set a Tomato Timer? Eat a Frog? Be Like Ike? Comparing 5 Common Productivity Systems," *Washington Post,* August 2, 2021. www.washingtonpost.com.

Rose Leadem, "17 Tricks to Get More Done During the Work Day," *Entrepreneur,* September 28, 2016. www.entrepreneur.com.

Alissa J. Mrazek et al., "Teenagers' Smartphone Use During Homework: An Analysis of Beliefs and Behaviors Around Digital Multitasking," *Education Sciences,* 2021. https://eric.ed.gov.

Britney Nguyen, "What Is 'Monk Mode': How the Viral Productivity Hack Works—and How CEOs and Entrepreneurs Use It," Insider, February 8, 2023. www.businessinsider.com.

Dana G. Smith, "How to Focus Like It's 1990," *New York Times,* January 9, 2023. www.nytimes.com.

Websites

American Institute of Stress
www.stress.org
The institute advances the understanding of the role stress plays in health and illness. Information about the effects of stress and stress management is available on the organization's website.

American Psychological Association
www.apa.org
This organization promotes the advancement, communication, and application of psychological science and knowledge. Its website contains articles about how psychology applies to daily life.

James Clear
https://jamesclear.com
James Clear, the author of *Atomic Habits,* features self-improvement tips and information about building better habits on his website.

Psychology Today
www.psychologytoday.com/us
News and articles about how psychology relates to everyday life are featured on this website. Topics include mindfulness, perfectionism, and motivation.

Verywell Mind
www.verywellmind.com
Articles about procrastination, stress management, and motivation are available on this website, which also contains information about mental health.

Time Management Apps

Some phone apps may help you manage your time and stay on track. These are just a few of the many that can help.

AntiSocial: The AntiSocial app reports how much time you spend in each app and compares your usage to others'. It gives you a score that assesses your phone dependence.

Forest: When you open the Forest app, you see a virtual tree grow while you focus on your work. If you leave the app before your focus time is up, the tree will die. The app partners with a real-life tree-planting organization, and users can spend virtual coins they earn in the app to plant real trees.

myHomework Student Planner: This app allows you to track assignments, grades, and projects as well as other dates and events. It includes a homework widget that sends reminders to keep you from missing deadlines.

My Study Life: Classes, assignments, and personal obligations can be tracked on this app, which uses a to-do list and color-coded tiles to help you organize your tasks.

Remember the Milk: This time-management app is designed for anyone, but it can help students organize their to-do list and remind them when a task is due. It also allows bigger tasks to be broken down into smaller pieces, and it can be synced with a calendar and email.

StayFocused: This app restricts the amount of time you can spend on websites that waste your time. After your allotted time is up, the sites are inaccessible for the rest of the day.

INDEX

Note: Boldface page numbers indicate illustrations.

Alamour, Rhonda, 19, 20
American Academy of Sleep Medicine, 8
American Institute of Stress, 56
American Psychological Association, 57
AntiSocial (time management app), 57
anxiety, 8
  mindfulness and, 50
  procrastination and, 14–15, 46, 48
  smartphones and, 35
Atomic Habits (Clear), 31
Attention Span (Mark), 42
attention spans, 5

backpack, cleaning out, 21
Becker, Joshua, 47
Bellur, Saraswati, 40
Big Thing, The (Korkki), 52
brain, **9**
  challenges/creative activities as strengthening, 13–14
  distractions and, 6
  emotional/impulsive part of, 7–8
  sleep and, 8–9
British Journal of Health Psychology, 11
Buehler, Roger, 27, 28

caffeine, 11
Canu, Will, 50
Carter, Sherrie Bourg, 23, 24

cell phones. *See* smartphones
Cirillo, Francesco, 40
Clear, James, 31
  website of, 57
clutter, as distracting, 23

daily routine, 4, 19
  as means of taking control, 17–18
difficult assignments/classes, getting through frustration with, 15–16
distractions, 34
  clearing work area of, 22–23
  resisting, 38–39
  silence as, 24
  from smartphones, 5, 6, 34–36

Education Sciences (journal), 5, 41
electronic devices
  sleep deprivation and, 9–10
  See also smartphones

Farnum, Amy, 24
Ferrari, Joseph, 44
Forest (time management app), 57

goals
  procrastination and, 48
  working toward long-term, 32
  See also tasks
Google Calendar (digital planner app), 19
Griffin, Dale, 27

headphones, as signal to not be disturbed, 38
Hershfield, Hal, 45
Hollis, Briana Mary Ann, 13
homework
  amount of time students spend being distracted from, 34
  multitasking and, 36–37, 40
  optimizing workspace for, 22–24
  resisting distractions from, 38–39
  smartphones and, 35
  tackling most challenging, first, 32
  using class time for, 25–26, **26**
Hoover, Sarah, 49
Hyman, Ira E., Jr., 37

Institute of Education Sciences, 34
Ivy Lee system, 30–31

JamesClear.com, 57

Kahneman, Daniel, 27
Kam, Julie, 43
Korkki, Phyllis, 52

Leadem, Rose, 36–37
Le Cunff, Anne-Laure, 29
Lee, Ivy, **30**, 30–31
limbic system, 8
long-term goals, 32

Mark, Gloria, 5, 6, 42
microproductivity, 25–27
mindfulness, 50
Morin, Amy, 17, 18

multitasking, 36–37
  cost of, 40
myHomework Student Planner (time management app), 57
My Study Life (time management app), 58

Okorie, Caroline, 9
opinion polls. *See* surveys
organizational habits, 14

perfectionism, 13
planning
  for long-term deadlines, 27
  prefrontal cortex and, 50
  procrastinators and skills for, 15
planning fallacy, 6, 27–28
polls. *See* surveys
Pomodoro Technique, 40–41
prefrontal cortex, 8
Price, Adam, 15–16
procrastination, 6
  chronic, 47–49
  as emotion regulation problem, 45–46
  impairs development of planning skills, 14–15
  as intentional avoidance, 44–45
  mindfulness and overcoming, 50
  overcoming, 49
  perfectionism and, 13
  two-minute rule and, 47
productivity
  effect of multitasking on, 37
  Ivy Lee method for, 30–31
  lack of sleep and, 10
Psychology Today (website), 57
Pychyl, Tim, 45, 50, 51

Remember the Milk (time management app), 58
Rizzo, Paula, 41
Rosen, Larry, 35
routine. *See* daily routine

schedules, **20**
   budgeting sleep time in, 11
   creating, 19–21
   long-term goals and, 32
   misjudging length of time to complete tasks and, 15
   random events as distraction from, 35
   sleep/wake versus school, 8–9
Schroder, Hans, 21
Schwab, Charles M., 30–31
Sirois, Fuschia, 13, 44, 46, 47–48
sleep, 8–9
Sleep Foundation, 10
smartphones, 4–5, **39**
   avoiding distractions from, 38–39, 41
   awareness of surroundings and, 37
Smith, Dana G., 35
social events, including in daily schedule, 20
social media, 14
   allure of, 4–6
   deleting apps for, 39
   discipline and limiting use of, 41
   as distraction, 34, 38
   ignoring, as source of anxiety, 35
   multitasking and, 36, 40
Solving the Procrastination Puzzle (Pychyl), 45

StayFocused (time management app), 58
stress, 7
   mental/physical health and, 48
   organization of workspace and, 22
   switching between tasks and, 6
   taking breaks and, 43
   writing as relief for, 21
surveys
   on restricting smartphone use during homework, 41
   of teens on smartphones and ability to concentrate, 5
switch cost, 6

tasks
   long-term, prioritizing, 30
   making plans for finishing, 29
   switching between, 5–6
   tackling most unpleasant, first, 31–33
   underestimating time needed for, 27–28
teens
   difficulty of, getting enough sleep, 8–10
   impulse control and, 6
   percentage of, believing smartphones impair concentration, 5
   percentage of, using smartphones, 34
13 Things Strong Kids Do (Morin), 17
time management, 6
   apps for, 19, 57–58
   finding best approach for, 33

improving work environment by, 22
planning fallacy and, 27–28
Tversky, Amos, 27
Twain, Mark, 31

University of Connecticut, 40

Vanderkam, Laura, 33

Vasireddy, Navya, 24
Verywell Mind (website), 57
Voices of Youth (blog), 12

Weinschenk, Susan, 37, 39
Wong, Daniel, 49
workspace, optimizing, 22–24
writing, as means to deal with worrying, 21

PICTURE CREDITS

Cover: Juice Verve/Shutterstock

5: fizkes/Shutterstock
9: Miha de/Shutterstock
10: Peter Snaterse/Shutterstock
14: DimaBerlin/Shutterstock
18: Monkey Business Images/Shutterstock
20: NicoElNino/Shutterstock
23: Slatan/Shutterstock
26: Slatan/Shutterstock
28: VK Studio/Shutterstock
30: FAY 2018/Alamy Stock Photo
36: Perfect Wave/Shutterstock
39: Thanik Boonthawornwat/Shutterstock
42: LightField Studios/Shutterstock
46: Oleksandr Nagaiets/Shutterstock
48: G-Stock Studio/Shutterstock
51: Lopolo/Shutterstock

ABOUT THE AUTHOR

Terri Dougherty is the author of more than one hundred books for children and teens. She lives with her husband in Appleton, Wisconsin. They have three adult children and always enjoy hiking, biking, and other outdoor activities whenever they can.